Books should be returned or renewed by the
last date stamped above

OLIVER, C

Life in a pond.

PEMBURY

Awarded for excellence
to Arts & Libraries

Kent
County
Council

# Life in a
# POND

Clare Oliver

Evans Brothers Limited

First published in Great Britain in 2002 by Evans Brothers Limited
2A Portman Mansions
Chiltern Street
London W1U 6NR

Copyright © 2002 Steck-Vaughn Company

Project Editors: Sean Dolan, Tamsin Osler, Louise John
Consultant: Michael Chinery
Production Director: Richard Johnson
Illustrated by Stuart Lafford
Designed by Ian Winton

Planned and produced by Discovery Books

British Library Cataloguing in Publication Data
Oliver, Clare
    Life in a Pond-(Microhabitats)
    1. Pond animals-Juvenile literature
    I. Title
    578.7'636
    ISBN 0 237 52300 0

Printed in the United States

# Contents

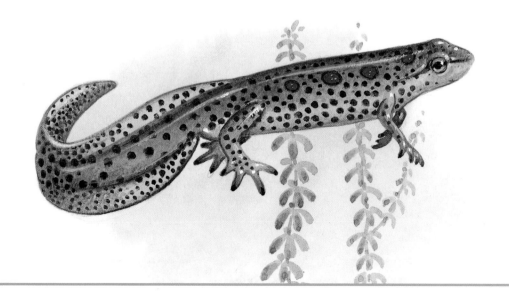

# A Freshwater Pond

## What is a Pond?

Ponds are small bodies of fresh water that are surrounded by land. They are like lakes, only smaller and shallower. Most ponds are not joined to another body of water, such as a river or stream and some are man-made. Unlike the water in rivers and streams, which moves or flows from one place to another, pond water is still. Pond water can become stagnant or smelly and even dry up. In winter, the surface of a pond can freeze over.

Moorhen

Frog

Water stick insect

Diving beetle

Tadpoles

Swan mussel

## A Busy Place

Ponds and the land around them are home to a whole range of plants and animal life, from algae to ducks and foxes. Some creatures just visit the pond to feed or breed, but many others spend their whole life there.

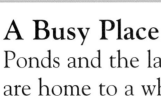

# Guess What?

In the 17th century, people accused of witchcraft were tied up and thrown into a pond. Sinking was thought to prove a person's innocence—even if they drowned!

The Hindu god Brahma was born on a lotus petal (the flower of a water lily). Buddha is often shown sitting on one.

In Japan, frogs are a symbol of good luck, especially for travellers.

Fox

Mallard ducks

Duckweed

Dragonfly

Whirligig beetles

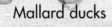

Water boatman

Pond snail

Sticklebacks

Water shrew

Newt

5

# Watery World

Life in a pond exists only because the water is not pure. It contains all sorts of microscopic inhabitants –just one cupful contains over a billion bacteria. The microscopic inhabitants of the pond are eaten by larger, but still tiny, creatures, which in turn become food for even larger creatures. This is called the food chain. This relationship between all the living things in a pond is what makes it a microhabitat, or an almost self-contained small environment.

Water fleas live just below the pond's surface. They are about 2mm long and are easily recognised by their jerky movements. The water fleas, which are crustaceans, are eaten by larger insects and fish.

# Food and Air

Under normal circumstances, the pond does not run out of oxygen because the plants that live in it constantly produce more. In a process called photosynthesis, plants take carbon dioxide from the water and light energy from the Sun to produce a sugary food for themselves. They give off oxygen when they do this. At night, pond plants cannot photosynthesise, and the amount of carbon dioxide in the pond increases.

Light energy from the Sun

Oxygen is given out by the leaves. Much of it dissolves into the pond water

Carbon dioxide is taken in by the leaves

Water is taken in by roots and submerged stems

## See for Yourself

The silvery bubbles on this Canadian waterweed are oxygen, produced during photosynthesis.

Seen through a microscope, a drop of pond water reveals all sorts of microscopic life.

7

# Plant Life

## Pond Plants

Irises, rushes, and grasses are frequently found near the edges of ponds. Reeds are aquatic grasses with flat leaves that sway in the breeze. They produce feathery flowers and fluffy seed-heads. The seeds take root in the rich mud and grow into new reed plants.

The shallow waters and boggy ground around a pond are home to a large number of plants, such as the purple irises and yellow marsh marigolds seen here.

## Life Adrift

Duckweed floats on the pond's surface. It has short roots that dangle from the tiny leaves and pick up minerals from the water. Other floaters include the amazing water soldier, which sinks to the bottom each autumn and floats to the surface again in spring.

## Guess What?

Water fleas and other tiny creatures should beware of the bladderwort plant that grows in ponds. It sucks them into traps and digests their bodies.

The sundew that grows around ponds also gets extra nutrients by catching insects. It uses sticky glue to trap its prey.

Common figwort smells terrible — but its strong smell attracts wasps, which pollinate it.

## Leaf Design

Plants that grow under the surface, such as hornworts and Canadian waterweed, often have feathery fronds for leaves. Leaves that open up on the surface, such as that of the lily, are broad, flat and waxy.

The broad leaves of the water lily provide shelter from the Sun for fish and other pond animals.

# Minibeasts

## Walking on Water

Some small, light pond creatures, such as pond skaters, can walk on water without sinking! This is possible because of surface tension – the force that pulls on the surface of the water, creating a thin, stretchy film.

Pond skaters spend much of the day darting across the surface of the pond in search of struggling flies.

Other bugs that flit about the surface include water crickets, which have orange-red markings on the sides of their bodies, and water measurers. The water measurer is very slender and walks slowly over the surface, looking for creatures to spear with its beak.

## In a Spin

Whirligig beetles are among the most unusual insects found on the surface of a pond. They whizz around in circles, using their short antennae to find prey. Their eyes are split in two, so they can look for prey or predators in any direction. The upper part of each eye looks above the water and the lower part looks below the surface.

Surface tension supports mosquito pupae as they hang upside-down from the surface of the pond. Many adult mosquitoes spread diseases.

## Insect Babies

All sorts of insect eggs hatch in the water. Some of the baby insects, or larvae, grow up to become insects that fly above the surface of the water. These include mosquitoes, dragonflies, midges, and caddis flies. Others, such as diving beetles, remain in the pond for their whole lives. Many young insects are fierce predators. Dragonfly larvae have spiked lower lips for spearing their prey, which includes other insect larvae, tadpoles and even fish!

This dragonfly larva is eating a worm that it has speared with its spiked lower lip.

## Guess What?

Some mayfly larvae spend three years in the pond, but less than a day as adults in the air!

Midge larvae include bright red bloodworms and see-through 'phantoms.'

The dragonfly larva breathes by sucking in water through the end of its digestive tract.

Caddis fly larvae build their camouflaged cases from leaves, plant stalks, grains of sand, or even old snail shells. They make sticky silk to glue the materials together.

## Caddis Case

With so many predators about, the caddis fly larva builds a case to hide its body. After about a year, the larva closes up the end of the case and turns into a pupa. This is the 'in-between' stage of its life, when its body changes into adult form. After two weeks, the pupa swims to the surface of the water or to the bank and splits its skin for the adult caddis fly to come out.

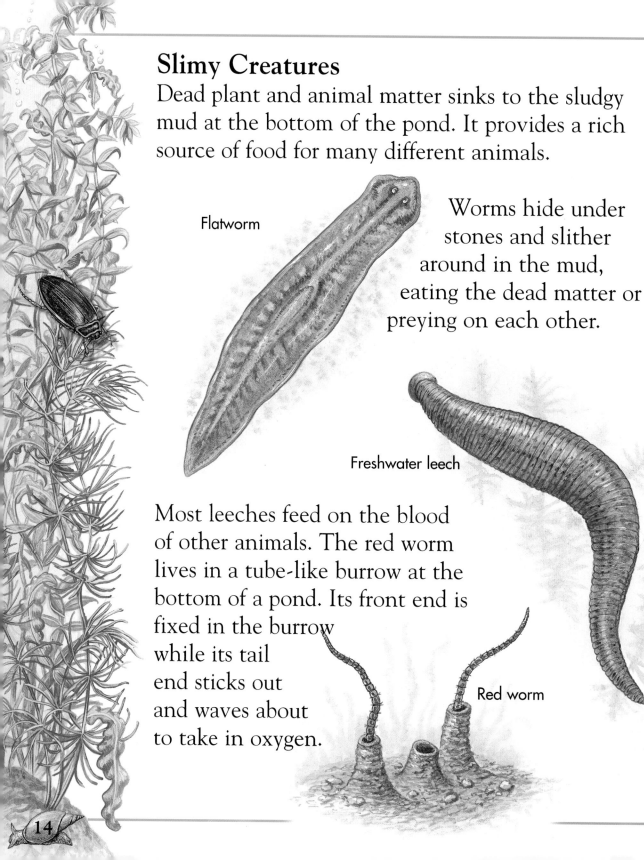

# Slimy Creatures

Dead plant and animal matter sinks to the sludgy mud at the bottom of the pond. It provides a rich source of food for many different animals.

Flatworm

Worms hide under stones and slither around in the mud, eating the dead matter or preying on each other.

Freshwater leech

Most leeches feed on the blood of other animals. The red worm lives in a tube-like burrow at the bottom of a pond. Its front end is fixed in the burrow while its tail end sticks out and waves about to take in oxygen.

Red worm

## Mussels and Other Molluscs

Freshwater mussels filter scraps of food from the water, while snails graze on pond plants and algae (plant-like organisms that do not have leaves, roots, or stems). Both of these animals are molluscs. They have soft, boneless bodies covered by a shell. Freshwater mussels range from the tiny pea mussel to the swan mussel, which grows to more than 10cm.

This pond snail is grazing on some waterweed.

## See for Yourself

In spring, look at the underwater stem of a plant. Strings of jelly-like capsules like this are masses of water snail eggs.

# Beetles and Bugs

Beetles are one of the most common insects found in a pond. They have biting jaws to chew up other animals and plants. Water bugs have needle-like mouths for sucking up food. Both freshwater bugs and beetles have hard cases to protect their wings.

The great diving beetle carries its own oxygen supply. It traps bubbles under its wing cases and can 'breathe' through holes called spiracles.

## Boating Bugs

The greater water boatman is a bug that swims upside down – that's why it is also known as the backswimmer. When it stops swimming, it floats to the surface for air.

Greater water boatman

The lesser water boatman swims the right way up and does not float. It has to swim to the surface to take a breath.

Lesser water boatman

## Other Bugs

Other pond bugs include water scorpions, water stick insects and saucer bugs, as well as the pond skaters, water measurers, and crickets that live and feed on the surface. Water beetles include the great and lesser diving beetles, which hunt fish and tadpoles, and the great silver beetle, which feeds on waterweed.

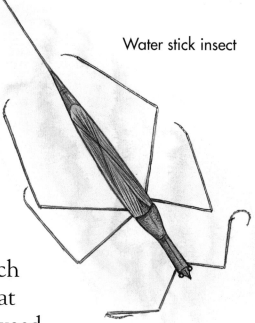

Water stick insect

# Bigger Creatures

## Underwater Animals

Amphibians are animals that can live on land and in the water. Pond amphibians include frogs, toads and newts. The animals spend their early lives as tadpoles in the water. As adults, they have very thin skins that can take in oxygen from both water and air. Frogs and toads lose their tails as adults, growing back legs for jumping and swimming instead. Newts keep their tails throughout their lives.

### The Life Cycle of a Frog

1. After 21 days, frogspawn hatches into hundreds of tiny tadpoles.

2. Newborn tadpoles have gills to take in oxygen from the water.

3. At about 5 weeks old, the tadpole's back legs have developed.

4. At 9 weeks, the tadpole looks like a miniature frog, except it still has a tail.

## Pond Fish

Big fish would soon finish the food supply in a pond, so the main types of fish found in a pond are tiny sticklebacks and minnows. Minnows are members of the carp family, which also includes goldfish. Pond fish often swim together in schools to confuse pedators.

The stickleback has sharp spines on its back to protect it from predators.

5. By 16 weeks, the tail has completely gone, but it takes 2 to 3 years for the frog to become an adult.

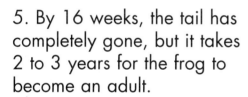

# Guess What?

The male stickleback's underside changes colour at mating time – it turns bright red.

A string of toad eggs, or spawn, can be up to 2m long.

The mudpuppy is an American newt-like amphibian that never really grows up. Unlike other newts, it keeps its feathery gills all its life.

# Pond Birds

The thick reeds around the edge of the pond make good, safe places for nesting birds, such as reed warblers and buntings. Swans, ducks and moorhens nest on the banks, and grebes often make nests that float on the water. Young birds soon follow their parents out onto the water – for example, swans can swim when they are just a few hours old.

These mallard ducklings are just one week old.

## Made for Water

Ducks and grebes waddle rather than walk because their legs are positioned so far back on their bodies. This makes them much better swimmers. Water birds also have extra-oily feathers so the water runs off them.

## Long Journeys

Ducks and geese living in the far north fly south when their homes start to freeze in the autumn. This is called migration. Many of them settle in Britain for the winter.

## Guess What?

Male swans are called cobs, females are called pens, and swan babies are called cygnets.

Weighing in at 23kg, the mute swan is the heaviest flying bird.

Mallard ducks don't just nibble weed. They'll gobble up a frog given half a chance!

These Canada geese do not really migrate and live in Britain throughout the year, but large flocks can be seen flying regularly between the ponds, fields and meadows in which they graze.

## Just Visiting

All sorts of other birds stop at the pond for a drink or a meal. Storks and herons stand patiently in the shallows for hours – then, as quick as a flash, spear a fish on their long beaks. Other visiting birds include kingfishers and the small songbird known as the dipper. Sometimes, highflying birds of prey, such as eagles or hawks, swoop down for a fish, too.

A heron uses its long beak to spear its prey.

# The Clever Beaver

Beavers can make their own ponds. If there isn't a pond or lake for them to use, they dam a river using branches, sticks, stones, mud or whatever else is available. These beaver ponds become habitats for plants, fish, frogs and birds.

Beavers are now extinct in Britain but can be found in Europe, North America and Asia.

## See for Yourself

The mud around the edge of a pond keeps a perfect record of pond visitors. See if you can find any of the footprints below (but don't stand too close to the edge):

- Fox or dog
- Duck or goose
- Moorhen
- Frog or toad

23

# Pond Hunters

## Dive-Bombers

Dragonflies and damselflies spend between one and three years living in the pond as larvae. The larvae are fierce hunters – and so are the adults! Hawker dragonflies fly around at about 30km per hour. They scoop up unsuspecting mosquitoes, gnats, or even wasps with their bristly legs. Darter dragonflies and damselflies prefer to perch on a reed, waiting for their prey to fly past.

### The Life Cycle of a Damselfly

1. The damselfly lays eggs on the plant stem.

2. After 5-15 days the larvae hatch.

3. The larvae stage can last between 1 and 5 years. The growing larva sheds its skin as it grows bigger.

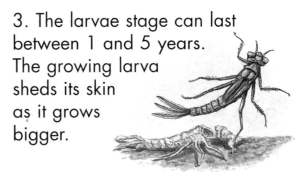

4. The larva climbs a stem, splits its skin one last time, and crawls out as an adult with crumpled wings.

## Hunters Hunted

In turn, adult dragonflies and damselflies provide a meal for birds such as wagtails and warblers or end up on a frog's sticky tongue or snared by a spider. If they fly too close to the surface, they run the risk of being caught by fish. Damselflies are also caught by the insect-eating plants called sundews.

Dragonflies and damselflies are insects. Their bodies are made up of three parts – the head, the thorax and the abdomen. They have six legs.

Head

Thorax

Wings

Abdomen

5. Adult damselflies mate in mid-air. Unlike the larvae, the adults may live for just a few weeks or a few months.

# Guess What?

Dragonflies eat in mid-air – and can eat their own body weight in half an hour!

In the days of the dinosaurs, some dragonflies were as big as seagulls!

Dragonflies perch with their wings spread, while damselflies bring their wings together over the abdomen.

## Turtles

Ponds provide a hunting ground for freshwater turtles, generally called terrapins. Musk turtles only grow to about 15cm, but they have a good way of driving away bigger predators – making a terrible smell! Snapping turtles are bigger and eat birds as well as smaller pond creatures and algae.

Of course, it would not be possible for all of these predators to live in a small pond at the same time as there would never be enough food!

## Furry Swimmers

Fur is a perfect body covering for pond mammals, such as water voles and shrews. Their fur is coated with an oily substance that keeps water out.

Water voles have been a protected species in the UK since 1998.

Voles are omnivores, which means they eat both plants and animals, whereas water shrews live solely on insects, tadpoles, frogs and fish.

Water shrews are really black and white, but bubbles of air trapped in their fur make them look silver.

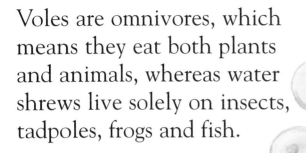

# Guess What?

The American alligator snapping turtle has a pink worm-like growth on the floor of its mouth that it uses to attract unsuspecting fish.

Shrews live very active lives but don't live for very long — usually only about 15 months.

Baby turtles have a special egg tooth. After they've cracked their way out of their shell, it drops off.

# Ponds Under Threat

## Upsetting the Balance

Ponds are balanced microhabitats. If a new species of plant or animal is introduced by humans, it can upset the whole food chain. The same problem occurs when species that already live in the pond are taken away by hunting or collecting.

The Australian waterweed in this pond is blocking out the sunlight. Other plants and algae in the pond need sunlight to survive and will die off without it. This, in turn, can affect the pond animals that feed on the plants and algae.

## Pollution

Pollution can destroy the pond's balance. For example, fertilisers sometimes drain off farmland into ponds. Once in the pond, they help the growth of algae. If there is too much algae, it covers the pond and blocks out the sunlight.

Farming affects ponds in other ways, too. Rain gradually carries soil away from fields and into the pond. Over time, the pond fills with soil, gets shallower and eventually becomes a marsh or a meadow. The spread of towns has also destroyed many ponds in rural areas.

## Unwelcome Visitors

Ponds are beautiful places for picnics, but visitors do not always take their rubbish away with them. This is dangerous as empty sandwich wrappers can trap small animals.

In many places, people throw away their junk in ponds. This can clog up the pond and cause damage to pond life.

29

# Glossary

**Algae:** Plant-like organisms, such as blanketweed, that live mainly in water. Like plants, algae use the Sun's energy to make food, but they are not plants because they do not have leaves, stems or roots.

**Bugs:** Insects that only feed on liquids, using a beak-like mouth to pierce and suck. An adult bug's front wings overlap on its back.

**Beetles:** Insects with strong jaws for biting. An adult beetle's wings are protected by hard, shiny wing cases.

**Camouflage:** Colouring, or a means of disguise, that makes an animal blend in with its surroundings so that it is more difficult for predators to see it.

**Food chain:** A series of plants and animals in a microhabitat that are linked because each one becomes food for the next one in the series. Large predators seem to be at the top (or end) of the food chain, but when they die their remains feed smaller, less complex organisms as well as new plants or algae.

**Larva:** An insect baby, such as a beetle grub, that looks nothing like its parent.

**Microhabitat:** A small, specialised environment, such as a freshwater pond or rock pool, where particular animals live and plants grow.

**Migration:** Describes an animal that regularly moves to a new home, usually according to the season. Geese and many other birds migrate, so they do not have to suffer harsh winters when there is little to eat.

**Molluscs:** Boneless animals with soft bodies that need to be kept damp and are sometimes protected by a shell. Freshwater snails and mussels are molluscs.

**Pollination:** The movement of male pollen to female flower parts to produce seeds. Plants might rely on wind, insects, birds or other animals to move the pollen.

**Pollution:** Damage to the environment caused by human actions. Chemicals that run off farmers' fields and into ponds cause water pollution. Exhaust fumes from cars are a type of air pollution.

**Predators:** Animals that hunt and eat other animals for food.

**Prey:** Animals that are hunted and eaten by other animals for food.

**Pupa:** The stage of an insect's life between a larva (baby) and an adult, when the body changes itself into its new form.

# Acknowledgements

The publishers would like to thank the following for permission to reproduce their pictures:
Front cover: Felix Labhardt/Bruce Coleman Collection; p.6: Colin Milkins/Oxford Scientific Films; p.8: Hans Reinhard/Bruce Coleman Collection; p.9: Bruce Coleman Collection; p.10: Kim Taylor/Bruce Coleman Collection; p.11: B.B.Casals/Frank Lane Picture Agency; p.12: Andrew Purcell/Bruce Coleman Collection; p.13: G.I.Bernard/Oxford Scientific Films; p.15: G.I.Bernard/Natural History Photographic Agency; p.16: Andrew Purcell/Bruce Coleman Collection; p.19: Kim Taylor/Bruce Coleman Collection; p.20: Dr Scott Nielsen/Bruce Coleman Collection; p.21: D.Maslowski/Frank Lane Picture Agency; p.22: Tom Leach/Oxford Scientific Films; p.25: Stephen Dalton/Natural History Photographic Agency; p.26: Stephen Dalton/Natural History Photographic Agency; p.27: Stephen Dalton/Natural History Photographic Agency; p.28: Roger Wilmshurst/Frank Lane Picture Agency; p.29: Martyn Chillmaid/Oxford Scientific Films.

# Index